The Life of a
TREE

Clare Hibbert

www.raintreepublishers.co.uk
Visit our website to find out more information about **Raintree** books.

To order:
☎ Phone 44 (0) 1865 888112
🖹 Send a fax to 44 (0) 1865 314091
💻 Visit the Raintree Bookshop at **www.raintreepublishers.co.uk** to browse our catalogue and order online.

First published in Great Britain by Raintree, Halley Court, Jordan Hill, Oxford OX2 8EJ, part of Harcourt Education.
Raintree is a registered trademark of Harcourt Education Ltd.

Editorial: Nick Hunter and Catherine Clarke
Design: Michelle Lisseter and Tipani Design
    (www.tipani.co.uk)
Illustration: Tony Jones, Art Construction
Picture Research: Maria Joannou and Ginny
    Stroud-Lewis
Production: Jonathan Smith

Originated by Dot Gradations Ltd
Printed and bound in China by South China Printing Company

ISBN 1 844 43318 8
08 07 06 05 04
10 9 8 7 6 5 4 3 2 1

British Library Cataloguing in Publication Data
Hibbert, Clare
The Life of a Tree. – (Life Cycles)
571.8'2216
A full catalogue record for this book is available from the British Library.

Acknowledgements
The publishers would like to thank the following for permission to reproduce photographs:
Alamy Images pp.**15**, **16**; Ardea pp.**13** (Duncan Usher), **14** (Geoff Trinder), **19** (John Mason), **23** (Francois Gohier); Corbis pp.**8** (Martin B. Withers), **10** (Tony Wharton/Frank Lane Picture Agency), **12** (Raymond Gehman); FLPA pp.**11** (Larry West), **22** (S & D & K Maslowski), **26** (Gerry Ellis/Minden Pictures); Getty Images (Imagebank) p. **28**; Holt Studios pp.**17**, **18**, **20**, **21**, **24**; NHPA pp.**9** (Rod Planck), **25** (Stephen Dalton); Oxford Scientific Films (Geoff Kidd) pp.**4**, **5**; Science Photo Library pp.**27** (Claude Nuridsany & Marie Perennou), **29** (Jeff Lepore).

Cover photograph of maple tree leaves, reproduced with permission of Photodisc.

The publishers would like to thank Janet Stott for her assistance in the preparation of this book.

Every effort has been made to contact copyright holders of any material reproduced in this book. Any omissions will be rectified in subsequent printings if notice is given to the publishers.

The paper used to print this book comes from sustainable resources.

Contents

Any words appearing in bold, **like this**, are explained in the Glossary.

The maple tree

Trees are very large plants. They have a sturdy trunk and leaf-covered branches that reach into the sky. The maple tree is deciduous, which means that it loses its broad leaves each autumn and puts out new ones each spring. When the maple tree is about 25–30 years old, it starts to produce flowers and fruits. This is its way of reproducing – making new maple trees.

In summer, this fully-grown maple is covered with green leaves.

Growing up

Just as you grow bigger year by year, the maple tree grows and changes, too. These changes make up its **life cycle**. This book is about the life cycle of the maple, but all deciduous trees go through the same basic stages.

Where in the world?

Sugar maples grow in cool, **moist** parts of North America. They have also been planted in parks and gardens in other parts of the world. Whole forests of sugar maples are grown for their sugary **sap**, which makes maple syrup, and for their **timber**, which is used for furniture.

In winter, the maple loses its leaves. Its branches are bare.

5

A maple's life

The **life cycle** of a maple begins with a **seed** lying on the forest floor. In spring, the seed starts to grow, putting out **roots**, a **shoot** and pairs of leaves. Each summer, the young tree, or **sapling**, grows a little taller.

The mature tree

When the maple is 25–30 years old, it flowers and produces winged seeds. In autumn, these seeds spin far from the tree on the wind. They may grow into new trees where they land. This happens every year for the rest of the maple's life, which can be 400 years or more.

Maple seeds start to grow in spring.

After about a month, the seedling has two pairs of leaves.

Over the years the maple grows into a tall tree.

Each autumn, the tree is covered with winged seeds.

From 25 to 30 years old, the maple produces flowers each spring.

This diagram shows the life cycle of a maple tree, from seed to tree.

Life begins

Maples drop their **seeds** in autumn. During the winter, the seeds are **dormant** – not active. In spring, the warmth of the Sun wakes up the seeds.

Springing into life

For the seed to begin to grow, or **germinate**, it needs water and warmth. The water comes from rain or melting snow. The warmth comes from sunshine. The maple seed does not need much heat. It germinates best at temperatures just above freezing.

This is what maple seeds look like when they are growing on the tree.

Root and shoot

The seed splits its outer coating and puts out a **root** and a **shoot**. The root pushes down into the soil to find water. The shoot pushes up towards the sky and sunlight. If it has to, a maple shoot may even struggle up through the last layer of snow.

On this maple seedling you can still see the winged case that contained the seed.

Extra sleepy

If conditions are not right during the first spring, the seed will not grow. A maple seed can stay dormant for several years. Then, one spring when there is enough warmth and water, the seed germinates.

First summer

Within a couple of weeks, the maple puts out its first pair of leaves. Leaves make food for the plant by combining **gas**, water and light. The gas is carbon dioxide, which comes from the air. Each leaf has tiny holes that take in the carbon dioxide. The water comes up from the plant's **roots**. The light comes from the Sun.

This way of making food is called **photosynthesis**. Photosynthesis would not be possible without a substance called **chlorophyll** in the leaves. Chlorophyll is what makes the leaves look green.

The seedling's leaves are like miniature food factories. They make food for the plant.

Growing season

During its first summer, the young maple grows to about 30 centimetres high. Its stem, which will one day be its stout trunk, is about 0.5 centimetres thick. **Shoots** grow out from the sides of the stem, too.

This sapling is a couple of months old. The straw covering the ground helps to keep the soil moist.

Shade lover

The **sapling** does not get much light. It is shaded by the fully-grown trees in the forest. Different trees grow better in different conditions. Birch, beech and maple trees, for example, prefer some shade. It is cooler in the shade, which keeps the ground **moist**, so that the trees' roots do not dry out.

First autumn

The maple's broad leaves are made mostly of water. In the icy, winter months, they would freeze and die. That is why the tree loses its leaves in autumn. First, it saves the useful parts of the leaf.

From green to red

Each leaf contains a green colouring, called **chlorophyll**. Leaves need this so they can **photosynthesise**, or make food.

The maple's leaves turn red before they fall in autumn.

The maple takes back the chlorophyll and stores it in its thin stem. Without chlorophyll, the leaves do not look green. They turn yellow, orange and red. The maple also stops sending **moisture** to the leaves. The stalks of the leaves dry out until the tiniest breeze will blow them off.

Leaf litter

Fallen leaves cover the floor of a forest in Autumn. Beetles, mice and other animals make winter shelters in this **leaf litter**. Eventually, the leaves rot down and return **nutrients** into the soil.

Squirrels collect leaf litter and use it to line their winter nests.

From sapling to tree

During winter, the **sapling** does not grow. It has no leaves to make food. For the rest of its life, the maple stays **dormant** each winter and grows taller each spring and summer. Slowly, its stem thickens into a trunk. Bark is the tree's skin. It protects the living wood inside the trunk. At first, it is shiny, smooth and grey – only older maples have rough, cracked bark.

Lost along the way

Not all saplings grow up into trees. Sometimes, animals nibble away the tender leaf buds and the sapling dies. Other plants are trampled down by animals. If every sapling survived, though, there would not be enough room for them all to grow in the forest anyway.

Damage from hungry white-tailed deer, like this one, can kill young maple saplings.

Mature maple

As it grows, the maple sheds its lower branches. The top part of the tree, where all the branches are, is called its crown. By the time it is 25–30 years old, it may be as tall as a house! It is still growing a little bit each year.

As it loses its lower branches, the maple forms its adult shape.

Sap rising

At the age of around 28 years old, the tree is ready to flower for the first time. Its trunk is now as wide as your body. Underneath the bark is living wood, or sapwood. In spring, this carries water and stored-up **nutrients** to the branches, so they can start to put out their leaves and flowers.

It is early spring. The maple's first leaves are starting to appear.

Sweet treat

The sweet **sap** flows up to the tips of the branches. Some birds have found that there is a sugary drink just under the maple's bark. Northern woodpeckers are nicknamed sapsuckers because they pierce the bark with their beaks, then suck out the sap. Sometimes, hungry hummingbirds visit holes made by sapsuckers to sip the oozing sap.

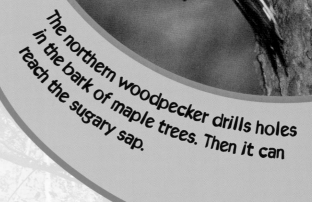

The northern woodpecker drills holes in the bark of maple trees. Then it can reach the sugary sap.

Maple syrup

People **harvest** maple sap in spring. They fit a tap in the maple's trunk so that the sap can drip out, down a tube and into a big container. Finally, the sap is boiled down to make maple syrup – delicious with pancakes!

Spring flowers

By April, the maple is covered with clusters of dangly, yellow-green flowers. Each cluster has between eight and fourteen flowers, each about the length of your middle finger.

The maple has male and female flower parts. Male parts produce a yellow powder called **pollen**. Female parts contain the flower's eggs, or **ovules**. To make **seeds**, the male and female parts must come together. This is called **pollination** and it happens in all plants.

The flowers appear on the ends of the branches.

Breezes and bees

Maples are mainly wind-pollinated. The wind blows the feather-light grains of pollen from flower to flower. Some of the flowers are pollinated by insect visitors such as bees. They come for the pollen, but some sticks to their bodies and later rubs off when they visit other flowers.

The spring breeze blows pollen from flower to flower.

Honey bees

Bees visit the flowers of many plants, including sugar maples and apple trees, to collect pollen and **nectar**. Bees use these to make honey and a special food called bee bread, which they use to feed their **larvae**, or young.

Leaf-covered tree

As the flowers fade, leaves appear in pairs along the tree's smooth, brown twigs. Soon, the maple is covered in bright green. Each leaf usually has five points, or lobes, and each makes food for the growing tree.

The maple tree's branches are now covered in leaves.

Leaf munchers

Some moths lay their eggs on sugar maple leaves. They include gypsy moths and leafcutters. When the eggs hatch, the tiny caterpillars feed on the leaves. Although they nibble away at the leaves, they do not cause a lot of damage. Even if some leaves are eaten up, the tree has hundreds more.

Mighty mites

Have you ever seen a **gall** on a maple leaf? A gall is a bump with a tiny, eight-legged creature called a mite living inside. The mite lays its eggs in there. Some galls can be really colourful – brilliant red or purple.

The bumps on this leaf are galls. There is a tiny mite living inside each one.

Summer months

Summer is the maple's growing season. Below the ground, its network of **roots** stretches further and deeper. Above the ground, new twigs appear on the branches.

Nesting birds

High in the branches, robins, bluebirds and other songbirds build nests from twigs. The birds help the maple. They feed their hungry chicks with the caterpillars that are eating the maple's leaves, and on other insects that are sheltering in the maple's bark.

This acadian flycatcher has made its tiny nest at the end of a maple branch.

Hollow homes

Other birds nest inside the maple's trunk. Woodpeckers use their beaks to hollow out the wood. Screech owls sometimes move into old woodpecker nests.

Life in the bark

The sugar maple borer is a yellow-and-black beetle that lays its eggs in cracks in the maple's bark. When the eggs hatch, the beetle **larvae** tunnel through the trunk, gobbling up the **sap** and wood as they go.

In their hollow home, a pair of screech owls may raise as many as six owlets.

Fruit

It is high summer. At the ends of the twigs, where the flowers grew in spring, there are clusters of horseshoe-shaped fruits. Each fruit, or **samara**, is made up of a pair of **seeds**, attached to two papery wings. The seeds grew out of the maple flower **ovules**. They were **fertilized** and began to swell after the flowers were **pollinated**.

These are clusters of samaras at the ends of the maple's branches.

Ripe and ready

It takes about ten weeks for the fruits to grow to full size, and another two weeks for them to ripen. By the time they are ripe, the fruits have changed from bright green to brown. Now the tree is covered with ripe fruits. In a couple more weeks, they will be ready to fall.

Pesky squirrels

Squirrels love eating the maple's seeds. They race from tree to tree, scampering to the ends of branches to pick the bunches. Squirrels have sharp teeth that make short work of the hard seeds.

This squirrel feasts on samaras all autumn. It needs to build up fat stores that will help it to survive the cold winter.

Spinning seeds

Every **seed** contains the beginning of a new maple tree. Now it is ripe, the **samara** needs to move away from the parent plant to a place where there is space to grow. This is called seed dispersal.

The deer mouse lives in forests in North America. It feeds on seeds and fruits and helps to carry seeds away from their parent plants.

Samara survivors

By early autumn there are countless samaras on the forest floor. Not all will survive the winter. Many will be eaten by mice, birds and other small animals, but some will **germinate** the following spring. Then, the **life cycle** will begin all over again.

Up, up and away!

The maple relies on the wind to carry away its seeds. First, the maple cuts off food supplies to the samara. This dries out the stalk so the samara can blow off the tree when there is a big gust of wind. Its wings spin like a helicopter's blades, carrying it through the air. The samara may land as far as 100 metres away – that is about the length of a football pitch.

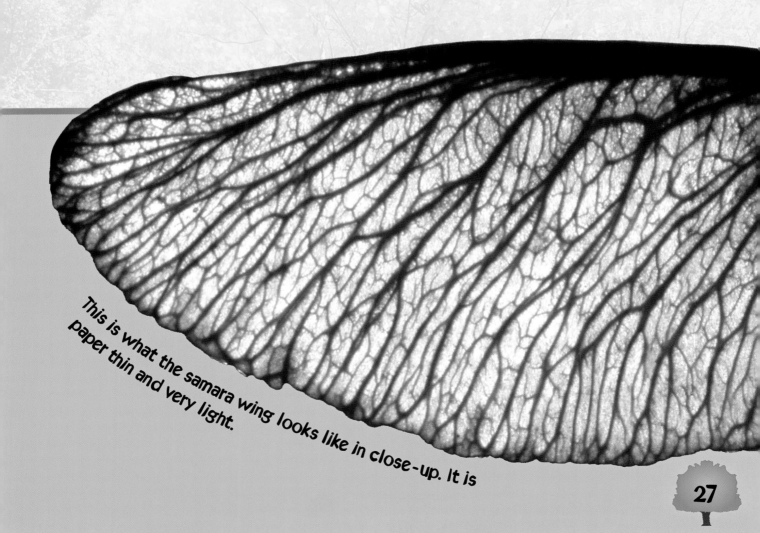

This is what the samara wing looks like in close-up. It is paper thin and very light.

Last years

By the time the maple is about 150 years old, it is as tall as a 6-storey building. It will not grow any taller now, but its metre-wide trunk will still get a little wider. Year after year, the maple carries on producing flowers, leaves and **seeds**.

When you see maple trees, think about what the world was like when they were just seedlings. Some maple trees are hundreds of years old!

The end of a maple

A maple can live for 400 years or more – but many are cut down before then for their **timber**. Eventually the maple dies naturally. The old trunk starts to rot. The tree gets weaker and might even snap over in a fierce storm. A dead maple is still an important part of the forest. **Fungi** and beetles can live on the rotting wood.

Fungi can grow out of the bark of an old tree trunk.

People and trees

As well as giving us wood and fruit, trees also produce oxygen – the **gas** that all animals need to breathe to live. Plants give off oxygen during the process of **photosynthesis**. That is why it is important not to chop down more trees than we plant.

Find out for yourself

The best way to find out more about the **life cycle** of a tree is to watch it happen with your own eyes. Look in your garden or visit local parks to see trees through the seasons. You can also find out more by reading books about maples and other trees, and by looking for information on the Internet.

Books to read

Eyewitness Guides: Tree, David Burnie (Dorling Kindersley, 2000)
I Wonder Why Trees Have Leaves and Other Questions about Plants, Andrew Charman (Kingfisher Books, 2003)
The Life Cycle of a Tree, Kathryn Smithyman and Bobbie Kalman (Crabtree Publishing Company, 2002)

Using the Internet

Explore the Internet to find out more about maples. Websites can change, and if one of the links below no longer works, don't worry. Use a search engine, such as www.yahooligans.com, and type in keywords such as 'maple', 'acer' (the tree's scientific name) and 'life cycle'.

Websites

http://www.alienexplorer.com/ecology/e128.html
Find out some more interesting facts about the sugar maple.
http://www.oplin.lib.oh.us/products/tree
Learn how to identify trees by their leaves, fruits or names.

Glossary

chlorophyll green colouring in plant cells that help it make food

dormant not active

fertilize when male and female parts join together to create the beginnings of a new living thing

fungi plant-like living things that do not have green leaves. Mushrooms are types of fungi.

gall growth produced by a tree around eggs laid by an insect

gas an air-like substance. Plants need the gas carbon dioxide, so that they can make food.

germinate when a seed begins to grow

harvest gather or collect something useful from a plant, such as its sap, leaves or seeds

larva young insect that looks nothing like its parent

leaf litter layer of dead and rotting leaves that lie on a forest floor

life cycle all the different stages in the life of a living thing

moist slightly wet

nectar sugary food that flowers produce to attract pollinating insects, such as bees

nutrient goodness that feeds a plant or animal

ovule female cell, or egg, that can grow into a seed when it has joined together with pollen

photosynthesis how a plant makes food for itself, using sunlight, water and air

pollen powdery grains that contain the male cells of a flower

pollination when male pollen from one flower is carried to another flower. This has to happen before a seed can start to grow.

root part of a plant that pushes down into the soil to suck up water and steady the plant

samara winged fruit of a maple tree

sap juice inside a plant's stem or trunk and leaves. Maple sap is collected to make maple syrup.

sapling young tree

seed small package produced by a plant that contains the beginnings of a new plant

shoot stem-like growth that comes out of a seed once it has germinated. The shoot pushes up through the soil towards the light, where it will be able to put out leaves.

timber wood that can be used for making things, such as buildings, ships or furniture

Index

Titles in the *Life Cycles* series include:

Hardback   1 844 43314 5

Hardback   1 844 43315 3

Hardback   1 844 43317 X

Hardback   1 844 43316 1

Hardback   1 844 43318 8

Hardback   1 844 43319 6

Find out about the other titles in this series on our website www.raintreepublishers.co.uk